THE BARON OF OTRANTO

Borgo Press Books by VOLTAIRE

The Baron of Otranto and Other Plays
Candide: A Play in Five Acts
The Death of Caesar: A Play in Three Acts
Oedipus: A Play in Five Acts
Olympias and The Temple of Glory: Two Plays
Saul and David: A Play in Five Acts
Socrates: A Play in Three Acts
Two Voltairean Plays: The Triumvirate and Comedy at Ferney

THE BARON OF OTRANTO & SAMSON & PANDORA

THREE PLAYS

VOLTAIRE

Translated and Adapted by Frank J. Morlock

THE BORGO PRESS
MMXIII

THE BARON OF OTRANTO & SAMSON & PANDORA

Copyright © 1986, 2002, 2013 by Frank J. Morlock

FIRST EDITION

Published by Wildside Press LLC

www.wildsidebooks.com

DEDICATION

To Mike Lidsky, My Dear Friend

CONTENTS

THE BARON OF OTRANTO 9
   CAST OF CHARACTERS 10
   ACT I 11
   ACT II 26
   ACT III 36
   ACT III 41

SAMSON 45
   CAST OF CHARACTERS 46
   PROLOGUE 47
   ACT I 53
   ACT II 62
   ACT III 71
   ACT IV 85
   ACT V 98

PANDORA 109
   CAST OF CHARACTERS 110
   ACT I 111

ACT II 119

ACT III 129

ACT IV 141

ACT V 148

ABOUT THE TRANSLATOR. 163

THE BARON OF OTRANTO
AN OPERA BUFFA

CAST OF CHARACTERS

THE BARON

IRENE

A GOVERNESS

ABDULLAH, a Turkish Corsair

PRIVY COUNCILLORS OF THE BARON

SQUIRES AND YOUNG GIRLS OF OTRANTO

A SQUADRON OF TURKS

ACT I
SCENE 1

A room in The Baron's Castle.

The stage represents a magnificent salon. The Baron is alone, dressed in a dressing gown, lying on his bed.

BARON:

(singing)

Ah! How bored I am!

I haven't yet had any pleasure this morning.

(rising and looking in the mirror)

This assures me that the days of my life

Must flow, flow without shadow of trouble.

I aspire to be rejoiced

By the least wish that I have.

Hola! My people, let me be forewarned

If I can have some pleasure.

(Enter a Privy Councilor in a huge wig, dressed in dead-leaf gown with a black cape, followed by petty squires and girls of Otranto.)

PRIVY COUNCILOR:

Milord, our unique wish

Is to see you happy in your barony;

For a lord like you, it's a unique destiny.

BARON:

Ah! How bored I am;

I haven't yet had any pleasure this morning.

(They dress him.)

COUNCILOR:

Today's the day heaven gave birth,

In this famous castle, to our adorable master.

We are celebrating this day with really brilliant games.

BARON:

How old am I?

COUNCILOR:

You are twenty-eight-years old.

BARON:

Ah! I've attained my majority!

COUNCILOR:

Barons,

At the age of their majority, have the most noble custom.

They are all wit, full of sensitivity.

When it pleases them, they make war on the Muslims,

Fleecing their vassals at their trembling orders,

Emptying their strongboxes, or cutting off their ears.

They don't undertake anything without bringing it to a conclusion.

They do everything with a single word, quite often none at all,

And when they are lazy, they are still marvelous.

BARON:

They always told me:

I was well brought up.

Now then, answer me, my privy councilor,

Have I lots of money?

COUNCILOR:

Very little, but you can take that

Of your tax collectors, and not even return it.

BARON:

And soldiers?

COUNCILOR:

Not one; but by saying two words,

All the peasants from here will become heroes.

BARON:

Do I have some galleys?

COUNCILOR:

Yes, lord; Your Highness

Has wood, a wharf, and, if he wishes,

Vessels shall be made: the Hellespont will tremble.

Your Majesty will be the sovereign master of the seas.

BARON:

I see myself very powerful.

COUNCILOR:

No one is more so than you,

You taste in peace this noble and sweet destiny.

You don't meddle in anything; everybody works for you.

BARON:

Being so fortunate, why am I yawning?

COUNCILOR:

Master, these yawnings are the result of a great heart,

Which feels itself above all its grandeur.

This fine day of festivity, this beautiful day of birth,

Celebrates its joy as well as its power:

And no question, Milord will have the complacency

To take some pleasure; since he wants to have some.

You will be harangued; that's the first duty.

The spectacles will follow; that's our ancient custom.

BARON:

Quite often, all this makes me yawn more.

Harangues especially have this marvelous gift.

O heaven! I see Irene coming to these parts!

Irene is coming to pay me a visit this morning for sure!

Let my privy councilors vanish right away.

Harangues are superfluous cares for me.

My cousin appears:

I won't yawn any more.

(Exit the councilors and enter Irene.)

BARON:

(singing) Beautiful cousin, beautiful Irene,

My languorous melancholia

Vanishes when I see you.

Love flies to your voice,

Your eyes inspire giddiness,

Your heart makes my destiny:

All that bored me, now interests me.

I am beginning to experience some pleasure this morning.

Why answer me in song, beautiful Irene,

In these parts a sovereign law is cherished,

Which neither king nor shepherd can set aside.

If they don't say much about it, it's only to sing.

You have a voice so tender and so touching.

IRENE:

Cousin, it's not timely for me to sing.

I have no wish to do it; they're weeping in Otranto.

Your privy councilors are taking all our money.

You don't think of anything, and they make you believe

The whole world is very content.

BARON:

I am with you; I put all my glory there.

IRENE:

Know that to please me, you must change.

You must correct an unworthy softness;

Without that: no marriage.

You have virtues, you have courage.

Nonchalance has spoiled everything:

They gave you only sterile lessons,

They mock you, and your laziness

Renders all your virtues sterile.

BARON:

My privy councilors—

IRENE:

Lord, they are cheats,

Who have given you evil lessons,

And who nourish your pride and silliness,

So as to better pillage the barony at their ease.

BARON:

Yes, they brought me up badly; yes, I've noticed it,

And I feel myself completely different when I see you.

They taught me nothing. Emptiness is in my head.

But my heart is full of you, and once full of my conquest

Will make me again pleasing to your beautiful eyes:

Being loved by you, I will become more worthy.

IRENE:

Then, milord, when your virtue's returned.

I will resume for you the voice I have lost.

(sings)

Forever I will cherish you,

With all my heart I will sing.

Charming lover, always love Irene;

Reign in every heart, but prefer mine.

Let time strengthen such a tender bond,

Let time increase my fetters.

BOTH TOGETHER:

No, I'll never be bored,

I'll love you all my life.

Love, love, hurl your darts

Hurl your darts,

Into my ravished soul.

No, I'll never be bored:

I will love you all my life.

(A great noise and shouts can be heard.)

IRENE:

O heaven! What terrifying screams!

BARON:

What tumult! What uproar!

What strange celebration, each runs, each flees.

(A Privy Councilor enters.)

COUNCILOR:

Ah! Milord, it's happened:

The Turks are in the town.

IRENE:

The Turks!

BARON:

Is this really true?

COUNCILOR:

You no longer have asylum.

BARON:

What's this mean? Where did they all come from?

IRENE:

This is what your privy councilors have produced.

BARON:

Go tell my men to resist.

I shall run to aid them.

COUNCILOR:

Milord, your grandeur

Must protect the decency of its glorious rank.

IRENE:

Alas! My governess and my ladies of honor

Are coming from all sides, all atremble.

(The Governess and the ladies of honor enter.)

GOVERNESS:

Ah! Madam! The Turks—

IRENE:

Ah! Poor innocents!

What are these cursed Turks doing?

GOVERNESS:

The Turks—I can't stand it anymore—

They spread through your apartment.

The Corsair Abdullah is carrying everyone off,

And pillaging everything;

They enchain at the same time, father, child, wife, and daughter.

Madame! Do you hear the drums—the outcries?

THE TURKS:

(at the back of the stage)

ALLAH! ALLAH! War!

GOVERNESS:

Madam! I am dying!

(Abdullah enters, followed by Turks.)

QUARTET OF TURKS:

Pillage, pillage, great Abdullah!

Allah, ylla, Allah!

Conquer all,

Kill all,

Rape all!

Allah, ylla, Allah!

ABDULLAH:

Don't massacre,

No, no don't massacre.

Enough, enough. Devastate everything,

But don't massacre.

Shackle,

Drink, violate,

Don't massacre.

(While they are singing, The Turks enchain all the men with a long rope, which they rap around the troupe, the end of which is held by a Levantine.)

BARON:

(chained together with two councilors in great wigs)

Irene, you see if, in this posture,

I am making a noble figure of a baron.

QUARTET OF TURKS:

Pillage, pillage, Great Abdullah!

Devastate everything,

Pillage, drink, violate.

Allah, ylla, Allah!

IRENE:

What! These nasty Turks are not enchaining the women!

How much honor is there in these villainous souls?

ABDULLAH:

(singing) O brave corsairs,

Scarecrows of the seas,

Let's go share,

Drink, possess.

To your devises,

I surrender the men,

And let them all know,

All the ladies are for me.

It's my custom,

All the ladies are mine.

TURKS:

Pillage, pillage, great Abdullah!

Allah, ylla, Allah!

IRENE:

(to the Baron as he's led away)

Go, my dear cousin, I flatter myself, I hope,

If this Turk is gallant, to get you out of this.

Perhaps you will say, by my cares restored,

That a woman is worth more than a Privy Councilor.

CURTAIN

ACT II
SCENE 2

Same as Act I, later that day.

IRENE:

Let's console ourselves, my nursemaid.

We must, with cleverness,

Correct, if we can, traitorous fortune.

You know the bizarre destiny of the Baron?

GOVERNESS:

Not at all.

IRENE:

The Corsair, heated by wine,

In the transports of joy, when his heart abandoned itself

Without being informed of the rank or name of anybody

Had, to enjoy himself, in the courtyard of the château

Assembled the captives, and through a new whim,

Made three of them draw lots for the work he would give them.

A grave magistrate finds himself kitchen help;

The Baron for his lot received muleteer.

These are, they tell us, the risks of fortune:

In Turkey this whimsicality is common.

GOVERNESS:

Can it be that a baron, alas! Is reduced to that?

And what is your place in the court of Abdullah?

IRENE:

I don't have any yet; but if I am to believe

Certain bold looks, that from the height of his glory

The impudent lets fall casually on me,

I will soon have a nice enough situation,

And I will make, my nursemaid, a very honest use of it.

GOVERNESS:

Ah! I've no doubt of it; I know that Irene is wise.

But, madame, a corsair is a bit dangerous.

He seems willful and the passage dangerous.

IRENE:

With no manners whatever he took the master's apartment.

"I am the master," he says, "and I have the sole right to be.

Wine, women, cash, all go to the strongest.

The Conqueror deserves them and the vanquished are wrong."

In this fine idea, his heart takes joy,

And for all the pleasures his good taste unfurls,

While my baron, a curry-comb in hand,

Shivers in the stables, and tortures himself in vain.

He's making the most beautiful ladies come here.

To do them justice, and to judge between them,

To expose their merit to the light of day, and exercise their talents

In the steps of the ballet, with postures and songs.

We are going to give him this little party;

And, if my eyes conquer his handkerchief,

I will use it to play him a trick,

Which will bring about the triumph of my glory and my love.

Already I hear his fifes, his drums.

Here are our enemies, and here are my rivals.

(The Levantines arrive, each giving his hand to a lady. Abdullah arrives to the sound of Turkish music, handkerchief in hand; the ladies of the castle of Otranto form a circle around him.)

ABDULLAH:

(singing) Come, come, tender maidens,

My sword makes you tremble.

My word, dear young maidens,

Please me, disarm me,

Make me feel even greater honor

To surrender myself to love,

Than raping all the earth

With the terror of war.

Come, come, tender maidens, etc.

IRENE:

(singing this air tenderly and with calculation)

It's to serve our adorable master,

It's to love him that heaven gave us birth.

Mars and Venus desired to form him.

His arm is feared, his heart is more loved.

From Cupid's tender mother,

Born on the breast of the waves,

To decorate our corsair

With her most beautiful gifts.

(she speaks)

Your handkerchief is the most cherished wish

Of the beauties of our barony.

But none has the right to be flattered.

She may please you, but she doesn't deserve you.

(Abdullah smokes on a sofa; the ladies present themselves in review before him. He makes faces at each one, and finally gives the handkerchief to Irene.)

ABDULLAH:

Grasp the handkerchief,

You richly earned it.

Let all the other maidens,

Less graceful, less beautiful,

Wait till later.

That's my sovereign will.

(he makes Irene sit beside him)

Sing to me, Irene.

And all the rest of you, go.

(they all go, bowing to him)

Fine, fine. they'll do,

For another time,

For another time.

ABDULLAH:

Dear Irene,

Now sit near me.

Love is goading me, consuming me.

(he makes her sit near him)

IRENE:

(beside Abdullah on the couch)

Lord, my soul is penetrated by your bounties;

I've never spent a more beautiful evening.

Before, when I feared the Turks, so proud in battle,

My heart, my tender heart didn't know you.

No, it's not with Turks you are comparable.

I thought that Mahomet was much less lovable.

And to complete these sweet pleasures,

I am counting on having the pleasure of dining with you.

ABDULLAH:

Yes, yes, sweetie, we will. Let us smolder together

Privately, one vis-à-vis the other, without slavery,

One to one, we will drink Greek wine, and sing, and play

With each other opposite each other; yes, yes, darling, by God.

IRENE:

After so many bounties, do I still have the audacity

To implore a new bounty from my Turk?

ABDULLAH:

Speak, speak, I'll do anything.

What you will, hurry, hurry.

IRENE:

Lord, I am a baroness, and formerly, my father

Ruled Otranto with his laws.

He was Constable, or Count of the Stables.

It's a dignity I've always cherished.

My heart is still so occupied with it,

That before supper, if you'll allow me to,

I'll go command, for a quarter of an hour,

Where my father commanded.

It's the greatest pleasure you could do me.

ABDULLAH:

What! In the pigsty?

IRENE:

In the pigsty, Signor.

In the name of tender love, I beg you again.

A hero like you, made for tenderness,

Could he harshly refuse his mistress?

ABDULLAH:

The lady is crazy.

The stables are stinky.

You will need a little flask of

Orange water to clean yourself.

Then, so as to give you pleasure,

I concede it; go, sweetie, and return.

(Irene leaves)

(singing)

Every young maiden

Clings to some fantasy

Resembling lunacy.

But my anger would be vain.

Enough, let the maidens

Be clever and pretty;

Everything will be excused.

Every young maiden

Clings to some fantasy.

CURTAIN

ACT III
SCENE 3

The stage represents a corner of a stable.

IRENE:

(sings) Yes, yes, I must hope for all;

Everything is set to deliver us.

Yes, yes, I can hope for all;

Love protects you and inspires me.

Your misfortune made me weep,

But by deceiving this Turk, that I am making sigh,

I'm ready to die of laughter.

BARON:

When you see me, curry-comb in hand,

If you were laughing it was with me.

I really deserved it; in my supreme grandeur,

Alas, I was unworthy of sovereign power,

And of the charming object that I love.

IRENE:

No, fickle fate

Has no power over my heart.

I loved you in grandeur,

I love you in slavery.

Nothing can humiliate us,

And when my tender lover becomes a muleteer,

I love him for it even more.

(she repeats)

And when my tender lover becomes a muleteer,

I love him for it even more.

BARON:

One must deserve such a perfect love;

Thus, as my fate changes in a single day,

Irene and my destiny awakes my courage.

(to his vassals who appear, armed)

Friends, sword in hand, let's beat out a passage

To our own hearths, ravished by these brigands.

Let's enchain, in their turn, these insolent conquerors,

Plunged in their intoxication, and delivering themselves

In prey to the security of their brutal joy.

You, guard this gate; and you, wait for me

Near my own room, at the top of these steps

Which give to the palace a secret entrance.

I will open the gate unknown to the public.

I want the corsair to be taken by my hand.

At the same moment, call with a great shout

All the good citizens to help their master.

Strike, pierce, kill, toss out the window,

Whoever dares to resist my valor.

(to Irene)

Goddess of my heart, it's too full to stop you.

Go to this party that the conqueror is preparing,

I am planning a rare dish for him,

And I hope this evening, happier than this morning,

To prepare the spit that that we're cooking for the villain.

IRENE:

I'm running, you see me at it, but let your tenderness

Not be shocked, if with some caress,

I deign to encourage his bold desires;

They are not, Lord, infidelities.

I think only of you when I tell him I love him.

Drinking with him, I drink with yourself.

By accepting his heart, I am giving you mine.

A little misfortune is often needed for a great good.

(Irene leaves.)

BARON:

(to his vassals.)

Let's get going, my friends, let's hurry to go to

The supper where Venus and Mars must await me.

Time is precious; I am running some risk

Of being a bit past master, and of arriving too late.

Do item by item what I prescribe.

Beware misunderstanding me, and let yourself lead.

Advance, feeling your way through this underground passage:

They will soon be the road to glory.

CURTAIN

ACT III
SCENE 4

The stage represents a pretty dining room. Irene and Abdullah are seated at a table without servants.

IRENE(singing, cup in hand)

Ah, what pleasure

To drink with her corsair!

Each cup that I swallow increases my desire.

Pour, pour, my beautiful lover:

Ah! How tenderly you pour

All the flames of love into my cup.

ABDULLAH:

Yes, yes, a toast to you,

Love, drink, laugh.

Yes, yes, a toast to you.

This vino from the Campagna

Resembles you,

Enchanting the whole earth,

Christians

And Muslims.

Beautiful, scintillating eyes,

By this foaming wine.

Yes, yes, a toast to you.

THE TWO TOGETHER:

Yes, yes, a toast to you,

Love, drink, laugh.

Yes, yes, a toast to you, etc.

(They dance together, cup in hand, singing)

Yes, yes, a toast to you, etc.

(The Baron, armed, and his followers enter the room from all sides.)

BARON:

Corsair, you must dance another dance.

ABDULLAH:

(looking for a sword)

Let's see! Let's see!

BARON:

Your master, and vengeance.

It is just, soldiers, to enchain him in his turn,

So to the end of his term, and all taken place in a day.

ABDULLAH:

Levantines, come!

BARON:

Corsair, your Levantines

Are all put in chains, and they are going to the galleys.

Friend, laziness ruined you, as it did me.

I am returning the lesson that I received from you.

And I give it to you again with thanks.

I am returning your vessel to you; go and leave with diligence.

Leave me the beauty that saved us all,

And embark my privy councilors with you.

(he sings)

I swear—I swear to obey

My beautiful Irene forever.

Fortunate people, whose sovereign she is,

Repeat with me, all happy to serve her.

CHORUS:

I swear—I swear to obey

My beautiful Irene forever.

                      CURTAIN

SAMSON
AN OPERA

CAST OF CHARACTERS

THE SENSUALIST

LOVES[1] AND PLEASURES

BACCHUS

HERCULES

VIRTUE

FOLLOWERS OF VIRTUE

SAMSON

DALILA

THE KING OF THE PHILISTINES

THE HIGH PRIEST

CHORUS

---

1. The French think of Amours or Loves as the pudgy little winged cupids seen in Baroque Pictures. There being no exact English equivalent, I've chosen to leave them as Amours, which sounds a little odd but still beautiful. FJM

PROLOGUE

The stage represents the room of the opera.

THE SENSUALIST is seated on his throne surrounded by PLEASURES and LOVES.

SENSUALIST:

On the fortunate shores embellished by the Seine

I've reigned long since.

I preside over charming concerts

That the Muse Melpomene gives.

Let leisure be born from the breast of indolence,

Spread your sweet errors

Pour into all our hearts

Your charming intoxication

Reign, spread my favors.

CHORUS:

(mimicking) Let's spread, etc.—

SENSUALIST:

Come, mortals, run before my eyes.

See, imitate the children of glory.

They've ceded to me Victory

Mars makes them cruel, and I make them happy

(Enter heroes armed and holding garlands of flowers in their hands.)

BACCHUS:

(to Hercules) We are children of the Master of Thunder,

Our name already renowned

Will never perish from the earth:

But let's speak freely.

Among so many laurels which gird your head,

Tell me that the conquest

Of Alcidas' great heart was the most flattering.

HERCULES:

Ah, don't speak to me further of my troublesome labors,

Nor of the heavens I supported.

In those parts I didn't know any except

Charming Iole and peaceable Pleasures.

But you, Bacchus, whose valor

Makes human blood redden the earth and the seas,

What pleasure, what barbarous honor

Do you find in troubling the world?

BACCHUS:

Ariane was never able to take from me

The memory of my brilliant crimes,

And with my helpful gifts

I ravish reason from wretched mortals

To make them forget all the evils I've committed.

TOGETHER:

Sensualist, receive our homage,

Enchant in these parts

Heroes, gods, and sages.

Without your pleasures, without your sweet advantages

Would they be sages and gods?

A LOVE (CHILD CUPID):

Jupiter isn't happy

From the crash of his thunder:

To your flames, Love,

He owes those precious moments

That make him so relish the earth.

The god who presides over the dawn

And who revives the world,

Would he make his vast tour

If he weren't going to find Love

Awaiting him on the crest of the waves?

Here all the conquerors restrict their grandeur to please;

Sages are lovers;

They hide their grey hair

Under the myrtles of Cythera.

Mortals follow the little Cupids

All wisdom is folly.

Profit from your good days

The gods will always be loving.

Be gods in your own lives.

SENSUALIST:

Ah, what dazzling light that pales the

Brilliance of the fine day that shines on us?

Who is this strict nymph that wisdom escorts?

CHORUS:

Let's flee cruel Virtue,

She banishes the Pleasures.

VIRTUE:

Mother of pleasures and of games

Necessary and often too fatal to mortals,

No, I am not your rival;

I come to join myself to you to better reign over them.

Without me, from your pleasures error is short-lived.

Without you, nobody listens to me.

My torch must light you

But I need your allure.

I intend to instruct and I must please.

Come, with your charming hand adorn Truth

Vanish, warriors consecrated by fables.

A true Alcidas

Shall appear in this place, enchanted like you.

Sing her glory and her weakness,

And let's see this hero vanquished by love

Once more adore Virtue

In the arms of tenderness.

CHORUS OF THE FOLLOWERS OF VIRTUE:

Let's sing,

Let's celebrate this day

The cruel dangers of love.

CURTAIN

ACT I

The stage represents a countryside. The Israelites are sleeping by the banks of the river Adonis deploring their captivity.

TWO CORYPHANTS:

Captive tribes

Who by these banks

Drag your chains;

Captive tribes

Whose plaintive voices

Reverberate in the air,

Adore in your sins the God of the Universe.

CHORUS:

Let us adore in our sins the God of the Universe.

A CORYPHANT:

Thus for the last forty winters

The indomitable power of the Philistines

Overwhelms us.

Their furor is implacable,

It insults the tortures we have endured.

CHORUS:

Let's adore in our sins the God of the Universe.

A CORYPHANT:

Unhappy and divine race,

Sorrowing Hebrews, shiver all of you.

Behold the frightful day that a mighty king destines

To place his gods amongst us.

Lying priests full of zeal and rage

Are going to force us to bend our knees

Before the gods of this savage region?

Children of heaven, what will you do?

CHORUS:

We will brave their wrath.

The Lord alone has our homage.

CORYPHANT:

So much fidelity will be dear to his eyes.

Sweet hope,

Daughter of Clemency

Descend from the throne of Heaven,

Treasure of the wretched;

Come beguile our troubles, come fulfill our wishes.

Descend, sweet Hope.

SECOND CORYPHANT:

(entering) Ah, already I see these cruel pontiffs

Who surround the altars of a horrible idol.

(The idol's priests in the cavity around an altar are revealed concealed by their gods.)

SECOND CORYPHANT:

Don't soil our eyes with these vain sacrifices

Let's flee these worshipped monsters.

We won't be accomplices of their bloody priests.

CHORUS:

Let's flee, let's stand aloof.

THE HIGH PRIEST OF THE IDOLS:

Remain, slaves,

Remain: your king in my voice orders you to.

Cowardly worshippers of a strange power,

Forget him forever, since he abandons you.

Adore the gods of his conquerors.

You will cringe in our chains, as your ancestors did,

Mutinous though conquered and always insolent:

Obey while there is time,

Learn the gods of your masters.

CHORUS:

Rather let the vengeance of heaven fall on us

Rather Hell engulf us!

Perish, perish

This temple and this altar!

THE HIGH PRIEST:

Refuse of nations, are you declaring war

On gods, pontiffs, and kings?

CHORUS:

We scorn your gods and fear the laws

Of earth's master.

(Samson enters covered in a lion's skin.)

SAMSON:

What a sight of horror!

What, these proud children of error

Have brought these monsters they adore amongst you?

God of battles, look in your furor,

The unworthy rivals that our tyrants implore.

Support my zeal, inspire me

Avenge your cause, avenge yourself.

HIGH PRIEST:

Profane, impious one, halt!

SAMSON:

Cowards! Conceal your head

From my just wrath:

Weep for your gods; fear for yourselves.

Fall, enemy gods! Be reduced to ashes.

You don't deserve for the god of battles

To arm the heavenly avenger, and thrust his lightning here.

My arm will suffice,

Fall, enemy gods! Be reduced to ashes. (he overturns the altars)

HIGH PRIEST:

Won't heaven punish this sacrilegious action?

Heaven is silent, let's avenge her quarrel,

Let's serve heaven by giving death

To this rebellious people.

CHORUS OF PRIESTS:

Let's serve heaven by giving death

To this rebellious people.

SAMSON:

Your astonished wits are still uncertain?

Do you still fear these gods overthrown by my hands?

CHORUS OF ISRAELITE WOMEN:

But who will defend us

Against the horrifying wrath

Of a king, the tyrant of the Hebrews?

SAMSON:

The God whose favorable hand

Has led this warlike arm

Has no fear of these kings of perishable grandeur.

Weak tribes, request his support

He will arm you with thunder:

You will be feared by the rest of the earth

If you only fear him.

CHORUS:

But alas, we are without arms, without defense.

SAMSON:

You've got me, that's enough; your misfortunes are over.

God has loaned me his strength, his power:

Steel is useless against the arm he intends to choose;

By taming lions I learned to serve you.

Their bloody hide is the noble forerunner

Of blows by which I will cause to perish

Tyrants whose image they are.

(air)

People, wake up, break your chains

Return to your first grandeur

As one day God on high

Will recall the dead to light

From the breast of ashes

And revive the universe,

People break your chains.

Liberty is calling you,

You were born for it.

Resume your allegiance

People, wake up, break your chains.

(another air)

Winter destroys flowers and greenery

But the torch of fecund days enlightens,

Revives nature

And renders it its beauty:

Terrible slavery withers courage

But liberty exalts its courage and nourishes its pride.

Liberty! Liberty!

CURTAIN

ACT II

The stage represents the peristyle of the King's palace; forests and hills can be seen through the columns in the back. The King is seen on his throne, surrounded by his court, dressed in the oriental manner.

KING:

So, this slavish people, forgetting its duty

Raises its unruly face against its king.

From the breast of ashes it braves my power.

On what fragile reed

Has it placed its hope?

A PHILISTINE:

An impostor, a vile slave,

Samson, has seduced them and braves you:

No question he is armed with the aid of hell.

KING:

The insolent one is still alive? Go, let him be seized:

Prepare everything for his execution:

Run, soldiers, load chains

On guilty Hebrews' vagabond troupe.

They are the enemy and the scum of the world

And detested everywhere, detest the universe.

CHORUS OF PHILISTINES:

(at the back of the stage)

Flee death, escape carnage,

Hell seconds his rage.

KING:

Again, I hear the screams of this mutinous people.

Are you going to punish the audacity of their odious leader?

A PHILISTINE:

(entering from the side) He is the conqueror,

He threatens us;

He commands destiny.

He resembles the god of war

Death is in his hands

Your overthrown soldiers embloody the earth

The people flee at his approach.

KING:

What are you saying? A single man, a barbarian

Makes my unworthy soldiers flee?

What demon declares himself for him?

(Samson, followed by Hebrews, brings in one hand a club, in the other an olive branch.)

SAMSON:

King, enemy priests, that my God makes tremble,

See this happy sign of charitable peace,

In this bloodstained hand

Which can immolate you.

CHORUS OF PHILISTINES:

What proud mortal can maintain this language?

Against a king so powerful, what arm can raise itself?

KING:

If you are a god I owe you homage,

If you are a man dare you brave me?

SAMSON:

I am only a mortal, but the God of the earth,

Who commands kings,

Who huffs at will

Either death or war,

Who holds you under his laws,

Who hurls the thunder,

Speaks to you through my voice.

KING:

Well! Who is this god? What is the testimony that

That he deigns to announce to me through you?

SAMSON:

Your soldiers are dying under my blows

The fear in which I see you, my exploits, my courage.

In the name of my country, in the name of the Eternal.

Respect, henceforth, the children of Israel

And end their slavery.

KING:

I, I should do such an outrage to the blood of the Philistines,

I, set free these odious people!

Your god must be more powerful than my gods?

SAMSON:

You are going to experience it: see if nature

Recognizes his commands.

Stones obey: let the purest waves

Pass through these rocks and fall back in torrents.

(Fountains can be seen pushing up.)

CHORUS:

Heavens! O heavens! At his voice, see spring up this ocean

Through softened stones!

The elements submit to him.

Is he the sovereign of the world?

KING:

Never mind what he may be; I cannot degrade myself

To receive laws from those who must serve me.

SAMSON:

Well, you've seen what his power is.

Learn what his vengeance is.

Fall, fire from heaven, ravage these regions,

Let thunder fall in bursts

On these fertile fields: destroy expectations.

(the whole stage seems to be inflamed)

Burn, harvests, dry out, fields,

Blaze up, vast forests.

(to the King) Know what his vengeance is.

CHORUS:

All is ablaze, all is destroyed,

A terrible god pursues us.

Burning flame, horrifying thunder,

Terrible blows,

Heavens, o heavens! Are we

At the day the earth must perish?

KING:

Suspend, suspend this harshness

Imperious minister of a god full of fury!

I begin to recognize

The dangerous power of your proud master;

My gods, long-time conquerors begin to give in,

It's their voices that decide me.

SAMSON:

It's his to command.

Having punished us, he is arming me with his lightning.

To your infernal gods go bring your terror,

For the last time, perhaps, you are contemplating

Your throne and their temples.

Tremble for them and for yourself!

(Exit King and Philistines.)

SAMSON:

You, that heaven consoles after such great wrongs,

People, dare appear in the palace of tyrants.

Let the trumpet sound. Organ of glory:

Blow, announce my victory.

THE HEBREWS:

Let's sing all about this hero, the judge of battles:

He is the only one whose courage

Never shares his victory with soldiers.

He's going to end our slavery.

Advantage is ours,

Glory's in his arm;

He makes tremble on their thrones,

The kings, masters of the universe,

Warriors on the field of Bellona

The false gods in the depths of hell.

CHORUS:

Blow trumpet, organ of his glory,

Blow, announce his victory.

THE HEBREWS:

The intrepid defender

Of a weak and timid troupe,

Guard their peaceful lives

Against the homicidal people

Who roar in deaf caverns.

The shepherd is resting and his flute sighs

Under his fingers to stretch its frenzy

With his innocent lovemaking.

CHORUS:

Blow: trumpet, organ of his glory,

Blow: announce his victory

CURTAIN

ACT III

The stage represents a grove and an altar wherein are Mars, Venus, and the Syrian gods.

KING:

Gods of Syria,

Immortal gods,

Harken, protect a people who shriek

At the foot of your altars.

Awaken, punish the fury of your criminal slaves.

Your people beg you

Deliver the most proud of humans

Into our hands.

CHORUS:

Deliver into our hands

The most proud of humans.

HIGH PRIEST:

Terrible Mars,

Invincible Mars,

Protect our territories.

Prepare

For this barbarian

Chains and death.

DALILA:

O Venus! Charming goddess

Don't allow these beautiful days

Destined for love

Be profaned by bloody war.

CHORUS:

Deliver into our hands

The most proud of humans.

ORACLE OF THE SYRIAN GODS:

Samson has subdued us: this glorious empire

Is drawing to its end;

Appease this hero: let him love, let him sigh,

Your only hope is in Love

DALILA:

God of pleasures, deign to instruct us here

In the charming art of pleasing and seducing.

Lend to our eyes your ever-conquering features,

Teach us to strew with flowers

The loving snare in which you wish to attract him.

CHORUS:

God of pleasures, deign to instruct us

In the charming art of pleasing and seducing.

DALILA:

Today is the feast of Adonis.

The youth are preparing for his games.

Love, now's the lucky moment

To inspire and to experience your flames.

CHORUS OF GIRLS:

Love, here is the time, etc.

God of pleasures, etc.

DALILA:

He comes full of wrath, and terror follows him.

Let's retire under this heavy foliage.

(she withdraws with the girls from Gaza and the priestesses)

Let's implore god who seduces

The most steadfast courage.

SAMSON:

(entering) The god of battles has led me,

In the midst of carnage,

Before him all tremble and all flee.

Thunder, the horrifying storm,

Do less to ravage the fields

Than his name alone has produced

Amongst the raging Philistine.

All those who wish to halt

This proud torrent in its passage

Have only irritated him.

They have fallen; death is their share.

(a sweet harmony is heard)

These harmonious sounds, these murmurs of waters,

Seem to soften my courage

Asylum of peace, charming places, sweet shadows,

You invite me to rest.

(he dozes off on a bed of lawn)

CHORUS OF PRIESTESSES OF VENUS:

(returning to the stage)

Flattering pleasures soften up his soul,

Charming thoughts, enchant his sleep.

GIRLS FROM GAZA:

Tender Love, enlighten his awakening.

Put in our eyes your power and your flame.

DALILA:

Venus, inspire us, preside over this gorgeous day.

Is this one here, the cruel, homicidal conqueror?

Venus, he seems born to embellish your court.

Armed, he's the God, Mars; unarmed, he's Love itself.

My heart, my weak heart, is timid before him,

Let's enchain with flowers

This terrible warrior;

May his wild invincible heart

Surrender to your sweetness.

CHORUS:

Let's enchain with flowers

This terrible hero.

SAMSON:

(awakening, surrounded by the girls from Gaza)

What sweet concerts are making themselves heard?

Where am I? Into what regions do I see myself transported?

What ravishing objects are coming to surprise me!

Is this the abode of bliss?

DALILA (to Samson)

We are celebrating the feast of charming Adonis.

Love ordered games for it:

It's Love who's preparing them,

May they deserve a glance from your eyes!

SAMSON:

Who's this Adonis that your lovable voice

Causes to resound throughout this beautiful abode?

DALILA:

He was an indomitable hero

Who made love to the mother of Love.

Every year we sing of this pleasant adventure.

SAMSON:

Speak, you're going to enchant me:

The winds have just stopped,

These forests, these birds, and the whole of nature

Become silent to listen to you.

(Dalila places herself at Samson's side. The Chorus forms around them. Dalila sings this cantatilla accompanied by small instruments)

DALILA:

In our regions, Venus often deigns to yield.

It's in our forests that one comes to learn

From her charming cult all the divine secrets.

It was near this sea, in these laughing gardens,

That Venus enchanted the most handsome of mankind.

Then everything was happy in profound peace.

The whole universe loved in the breast of leisure,

Venus gave the world

The example of pleasure.

SAMSON:

How alluring are her features! How her voice interests me!

How astonished I am to feel her tenderness!

With what a charming poison I feel myself penetrated!

DALILA:

Without Venus, without Love,

What would he have been able to pretend?

In our woods he is adored.

When he was formidable, he was unknown;

He became a god after he became tender.

Since that happy day

This place, this ocean, this shade,

Inspire the most tender love

In the most savage heart.

SAMSON:

O heaven, o unknown troubles!

I was that savage heart, and I no longer am.

I am changed, I am experiencing a burgeoning flame.

(to Dalila)

Ah, if there was a Venus,

If the loves of this charming queen

Could indeed present themselves to mortals,

I would take you for her, and think to flatter her.

DALILA:

I could imitate Venus' tenderness.

Happy is he who can burn with the fires she has experienced,

But I would have loved another than Adonis

If I had been the goddess.

THE HEBREWS:

(entering) Don't dally any longer, come:

A whole faithful people

Is ready to march under your orders,

Be the first of our kings;

Battle and rule: glory calls you.

SAMSON:

I am with you: I must do it, I accept your presents.

Ah, what powerful charm is stopping me!

Ah! At least defer, defer for a while,

These brilliant honors that you are offering me.

CHORUS OF GIRLS FROM GAZA:

Remain, preside at our festivals;

Let our hearts be here your conquests.

DALILA:

Forget battles,

Let peace attract you.

Venus is coming to smile on you,

Love extends her arms to you.

THE HEBREWS:

Beware the deceiving pleasure

In which your great heart is abandoning itself:

Love often steals from us

The treasures glory gives us.

CHORUS OF GIRLS:

Remain, preside at our festivals,

Let our hearts be your tender conquests.

TWO HEBREWS:

Come, come, don't dally.

Our cruel enemies are ready to surprise us;

Nothing can protect us

Except your invincible arm.

CHORUS OF GIRLS:

Remain, preside at our festivals,

Let our hearts be your tender conquests.

SAMSON:

I'm tearing myself away from these parts.

Let's go, I follow your steps.

Priestess of Venus, you, her brilliant image,

I'm not leaving your attractions

For the throne of kings, for that great slavery;

I'm leaving them for battles.

DALILA:

Must I long bewail your absence?

SAMSON:

Let your eyes trust my impatience,

Is there a greater good than that of seeing you?

The Hebrews have only me for their unique expectation,

And you are my only hope.

(Samson leaves with the Hebrews.)

DALILA:

He's moving away, he's leaving me, he's carrying off my soul;

Everywhere he's conqueror:

The fire that I lit enflames me;

I wanted to enchain him, he's enchaining my heart.

O mother of pleasures, the heart of your priestess

Must be full of you, must always self-enflame!

O Venus, my sole goddess,

Tenderness is my law, my duty is to love.

Echo, wandering voice,

Flighty inhabitant

Of this beautiful abode,

Echo, monument of love,

Tell of my weakness to heroes who enchant me.

Favorite of spring, of love, of breezes,

Birds whose concerts I hear,

Dear confidants of my extreme tenderness,

Sweet warbling of birds,

Faithful voices of echoes,

Repeat forever:

I love him, I love him.

CURTAIN

ACT IV

THE HIGH PRIEST:

Yes, the king grants you this terrible hero,

But you understand at what price:

Discover the secret of his invincible strength,

That commands the astonished world;

A tender marriage, a peaceful fate

Depend on the secret you shall have learned.

DALILA:

What can he hide from me? He loves me:

Only the indifferent are discreet:

Samson will tell me; I judge it by myself

Love has no secrets.

(Exit the High Priest.)

DALILA:

Help me, tender Loves

Bring peace to the earth;

Cease, drums and trumpets

To announce funereal war:

Shine, glorious day, the most beautiful of my life.

Marriage, Love, let your torches light it:

That ever I may please,

Because I feel that I will always love!

Second me, tender Loves

Bring peace to the earth.

SAMSON:

(entering) I've saved the Hebrews

Through the strength of my arm,

And you save through your allure

Your people and even your king:

It's for you to obtain the peace I grant.

The king is offering me his diadem,

And I want only you as the prize for my good deeds.

DALILA:

All fear you in these parts; they rush to please you.

You reign over your enemies:

But of all the subjects you've just made

My heart is the most submissive to you.

SAMSON AND DALILA:

(together) Let's no longer hear the noise of arms;

Amorous myrtle entwine with our laurels,

Love is the prize of warriors

And glory has more charms.

SAMSON:

Marriage must unite us with eternal knots.

Why do you still delay?

Come, let a pure love lead you to altars

Of the god of battles I adore.

DALILA:

Ah, let's tie these sweet knots in the temple of Venus.

SAMSON:

No, her cult is impious, and my law condemns it;

No, I cannot enter this profane temple.

DALILA:

If you love me it no longer is.

Stop, look at this pleasant abode,

It's the temple of the universe;

All mortals, at all ages, at all times,

Come here to ask for chains.

Stop, look at this pleasant abode,

It's the temple of the universe.

(The temple of Venus appears in all its splendor.)

DALILA:

(air) Love, sensual, pure,

Soul of nature,

Master of elements,

The universe is not formed, not vivified, and doesn't endure

Except through your beneficent glance.

Tender Venus, the whole universe implores you,

All is nothing without your fires!

They fear the other gods, it's you they adore:

They reign over the world, and you reign over them.

WARRIORS:

Venus, our proud courage,

In bloodshed, in carnage,

Vainly hardens itself;

You disarm us,

We surrender our weapons,

Horror softens at your voice.

A PRIESTESS:

Sing, birds, sing: your tender warbling

Is the voice of pleasures.

Sing, Venus must hear you,

Carry to her our sighs.

The daughters of Flora

Rush to blossom

In this abode;

The shining bloom

Of the burgeoning flower

Passes in a day:

But one more beautiful

Born near it

Pleases in its turn;

Sensitive image

Of pleasures of the prime of life,

Sensitive image

Of charming Love!

SAMSON:

I no longer resist: the charm which obsesses me

Tyrannizes my heart, intoxicates all my senses:

Possess forever this heart which possesses you,

And govern all my moments.

Come: you are confused—

DALILA:

Heaven! What am I going to tell him?

SAMSON:

What causes your heart to sigh?

DALILA:

I fear of displeasing you, and I must speak to you.

SAMSON:

Ah! Before you, it's for me to tremble.

Speak, what do you want?

DALILA:

This love which engages me,

Makes my glory and my happiness,

But I require a new proof

Which will assure me of your heart.

SAMSON:

Say it, all is possible.

To this amorous heart.

DALILA:

Tell me by what lucky charm,

By what secret power this invincible strength—?

SAMSON:

What are you asking of me? That's a terrible secret

Between heaven and me.

DALILA:

So, you suspect my faith,

You suspect, and you love me!

SAMSON:

My heart is very sensitive;

But don't impose on me this funereal power any further.

DALILA:

A heart lacking trust is a heart lacking tenderness.

SAMSON:

Don't abuse my weakness to such a degree.

DALILA:

Cruel! What an unjust refusal!

Our marriage depends on it; our knots will be broken.

SAMSON:

What are you saying?

DALILA:

Speak, it's love that's begging you.

SAMSON:

Ah! Cease to listen to this funereal craving.

DALILA:

Cease to overwhelm me with outraging refusals.

SAMSON:

Well, you wish it! Love justifies me:

My hair was long ago consecrated to my God.

They are the sacred guarantee of his bounties to me:

He wanted to attach to my strength and my courage

To such a weak decoration:

They are his: my glory is his work.

DALILA:

This hair, you say?

SAMSON:

What have I said? Misfortune!

My reason returns; I shiver

At the abyss to which I've dragged the Hebrews and myself.

THE TWO TOGETHER:

The earth roars, heaven thunders,

The temple disappears, the day-star flees,

Horror weighs on the night,

That with its terrifying veil surrounds me.

SAMSON:

I have betrayed my God's formidable secret.

Love! Fatal sensuality!

It's you who precipitated me

Into a frightful trap.

And I feel that God has left me.

THE HIGH PRIEST OF THE PHILISTINES:

(entering with Philistines)

Come, this terrifying uproar, these screams of nature

This thunder, all assures us,

That he's been abandoned by the god of battles.

DALILA:

What are you doing, perjured people?

SAMSON:

What! By my enemies I'm surrounded!

(he fights)

Fall, tyrants.

PHILISTINES:

Give up, slave.

(together)

Let's fight the enemy who braves us.

DALILA:

Stop, cruel ones, stop;

Turn your cruelties on me.

SAMSON:

Fall, tyrants.

PHILISTINES:

(fighting) Give up, slave.

SAMSON:

Ah! What mortal languor!

My hand can no longer bear this fatal sword.

Ah, God! My valor is deceived,

God withdraws his conquering arm.

PHILISTINES:

Let's strike the enemy who braves us:

He is vanquished. Give up, slave.

SAMSON:

(in their hands) No, cowards, no.

This arm is not vanquished by you.

It's God who delivers me to your blows. (They drag him off)

DALILA:

O despair! O tortures! O tenderness!

Cruel king! Inhumane people!

O Venus, deceitful deity!

You abused my weakness.

You prepared, through my fatal hands,

The horrible abyss into which I've dragged him.

You made me love the greatest of mankind

To hasten his death and mine.

Fall throne, burn altars.

Be reduced to ashes.

Horrifying tyrants, cruel gods,

May a more powerful god destroy with his lightning

You and your criminal race!

CHORUS:

(at the back of the stage) Let him perish,

Let him fall in sacrifice

To our gods.

DALILA:

Barbaric voices! Odious screams!

Let's go share his torture.

CURTAIN

ACT V

Samson in chains surrounded by guards.

SAMSON:

Deep abysses of the earth,

Hell, open wide!

Strike, thunder,

Destroy me!

My arm refuses to serve my courage;

I am vanquished, I am enslaved.

I will never see you again, sacred torch of heavens:

Light, you flee my eyes,

Light, brilliant image

Of your author, God,

First work of the Creator

Sweet light,

Sweet light

All of nature,

With veils of night's impenetrable horror

You hide from my sad eyelids.

Deep abysses, etc.

HEBREWS of THE CHORUS:

Alas! We bring to you our enchained tribes

Unlucky companions

Of your horrible sorrow.

SAMSON:

Holy people, unlucky race,

My arm exalted your grandeur;

My weakness has made your disgrace.

What! Dalila flees me! Dear friends, pardon

For such shameful unease.

CHARACTERS OF THE CHORUS:

She ended her unfortunate life,

Let's forget, forever, the cause of our tears.

SAMSON:

What! I undergo a new misfortune!

The one I adore is in the tomb!

Deep abysses of the earth,

Hell, open wide!

Strike, thunder,

Destroy me!

SAMSON and TWO CORYPHANTS (trio):

Love, tyrant that I detest,

You destroy Virtue, you drag behind your steps

Error, crime, death!

Much happier are those who do not know

Your pleasant and funereal power!

A CORYPHANT:

Your cruel enemies are advancing towards this place.

They are coming to insult the destiny which rushes on us.

They dare to impute to the power of their gods

The frightful ills in which God has left us.

(The King and The Philistines enter.)

KING:

Raise your voices towards your favorable gods,

Avenge their altars, avenge us.

CHORUS OF PHILISTINES:

Raise our voices, etc.

CHORUS OF ISRAELITES:

Let's end our deplorable lives.

SAMSON:

O God of vengeance! They are not guilty

Turn your blows on me.

CHORUS OF PHILISTINES:

Let's raise our voices

Towards our favorable gods,

Let's avenge their altars, let's avenge ourselves.

SAMSON:

O God! Forgive—

CHORUS OF PHILISTINES:

Let's avenge ourselves.

KING:

Let's invent, if it can be done, a new punishment;

Let the mark of death, suspended over his head,

Threaten him still and stop;

Let Samson in his rage hear our celebration,

Let our pleasures be his torture.

(Priests and Priestesses enter.)

A PRIESTESS:

All our gods stunned and hidden in the heavens

Could not save our empire:

Venus with a smile

Rendered us victorious:

Mars flew off, guided by her,

In his all-bloody chariot.

Immortal Victory

Drew out her shimmering sword

Against an entire faithless people

And eternal night

Is going to devour their speechless and trembling leader.

ANOTHER:

It's Venus who forbids storms

To growl on our heads.

Our cruel enemy

Still can hear our celebrations

Trembling at our conquests

And falling before her altar.

KING:

Well, what's become of this so formidable god

Who by your hands was going to slay us with lightning?

A woman conquered this terrifying ghost

And his languishing arm cannot be unfurled.

He abandons you, he gives you to my power.

And while in these parts I enchain destiny

His thunder, stuffed in his feeble hands

Reposes in silence.

SAMSON:

Great God! I've borne this horrible language

So long as he only offended a mortal:

He insults your name, your cult, your altar.

Arise and avenge this outrage.

CHORUS OF PHILISTINES:

Your shouts, your screams are no longer heard.

Wretch, your god is no more.

SAMSON:

You can still arm this unfortunate hand,

Grant me, at least, a glorious death.

KING:

No, you must feel through long draughts

The bitterness of your torture.

So that with you, your god perishes,

And that he will be, like you, scorned forever.

SAMSON:

You inspire me at last: it's on you that I found

My superb plans:

You are inspiring me: your arm is seconding

My languishing hands.

KING:

Vile slave, what are you daring to say?

Ready to die in torture,

Can you indeed threaten this formidable empire

In your last moments?

Let him be immolated; it is time;

Strike; he must expire.

SAMSON:

Stop: I must instruct you

In the secrets of my people and in the God that I serve:

This moment must serve as an example to the universe.

KING:

Speak, teach us all your crimes:

Deliver to us all our victims.

SAMSON:

King: order that the Hebrews

Be taken from your presence and this horrifying temple.

KING:

You will be satisfied.

(The Hebrews are led off.)

SAMSON:

The court which surrounds you

Your priests and your warriors—are they around you?

KING:

They are all here, explain yourself.

SAMSON:

Am I near that column

That sustains this abode so dear to the Philistines?

KING:

Yes, you are touching it with your hands.

SAMSON:

(shaking the columns) Odious temple!

Let your walls be overthrown,

Let your debris be dispersed

Over me, over this infuriated people!

CHORUS:

All are falling, all are perishing.

O Heaven! O God of Vengeance!

SAMSON:

I mend my shame and I die conquering.

CURTAIN

PANDORA

CAST OF CHARACTERS

PROMETHEUS, son of Heaven and Earth, a demi-god

PANDORA

JUPITER

MERCURY

NEMESIS

NYMPHS

TITANS

CELESTIAL DIVINITIES

INFERNAL DIVINITIES

ACT I

The stage represents a countryside with mountains in the distance.

PROMETHEUS:

Product of my hands, charm that I caused to be born

I call you in vain, you don't hear me:

Pandora, you cannot know

Either my love or your allure.

What! I formed your heart and you are not sensitive!

Your beautiful eyes cannot see me!

A pitiless power

Opposes all my wishes with an invincible strength;

Your beauty causes my despair.

What! All nature around you breathes!

Birds, tender birds, you sing, you love

And I see her allures languishing inanimate

Death holds them under its sway.

(Enter Enceladus, Typhon, and Titans.)

ENCELADUS AND TYPHON:

Child of the earth and the heavens

Your wails and screams have moved this grove.

Speak: which one of these gods

Has dared to do you some outrage?

PROMETHEUS:

(pointing to Pandora)

Jupiter is jealous of my divine work;

He fears that this object will be worshiped one day;

He cannot, without wrath, see the earth embellished;

Jupiter has refused life to Pandora!

He causes me eternal pain.

TYPHON:

Jupiter? What! It's he who would form our souls?

The usurper of the heavens may be our support?

No, I feel that life and its divine flames

Don't come from him.

ENCELADUS:

(pointing to Typhon and his brothers)

Our ancestors are Night and Tartary.

Let's invoke eternal Night:

She comes before shining Day.

Let Olympus give in to Tenare.

TYPHON:

May Hell, may my gods, spread among us

The eternal seed of life:

Let Jupiter shiver with envy,

And be vainly jealous of it.

PROMETHEUS AND THE TWO TITANS:

Hear us, gods of profound night,

From our new stars, contemplate the light;

Rush from the world's core:

Render fertile

The earth that bore me;

Give life to beauty,

Let your power

Second my happy boldness!

PROMETHEUS:

In the abode of the night your voices burst out,

Day pales, earth trembles,

The world totters, Erebus assembles.

(The scene changes and represents Chaos. All the gods of Hell come on stage.)

CHORUS OF INFERNAL GODS:

We detest

The eternal light.

We await

In our deep chasms

That weak and criminal race

Yet to be born, but that we hate.

NEMESIS:

The oceans of Lethe, the flames of Tartarus

Must ravage all things.

Speak, who do you want to plunge

Into the depths of Tenare?

PROMETHEUS:

I want to serve the earth, and not to oppress it.

Alas! I gave birth to this object

And I request in vain that it be vivified, that it think,

That it be happy, and that it experience love.

THE THREE PARCAE:

Our glory is to destroy,

Our power is to injure.

Such is the decree of fate

Heaven gives life and we give death.

PROMETHEUS:

In that case, flee forever this fine day that lightens me.

You are malefactors, you are not my gods.

Flee, odious destroyers

Of all the good I want to do;

Gods of malefactors, gods of crimes,

Funereal enemies,

Dive back into your shadows,

Leave the world in peace.

NEMESIS:

Tremble, tremble for yourself;

Fear our return,

Fear Pandora and Love.

The supreme moment

Flies on your heels.

We are going to unchain the demon of battles.

We will open the gates of death.

Tremble, tremble for yourself.

(The gods of Hell vanish. The countryside can be seen illuminated and pleasant. The wood and field nymphs are on both sides of the stage.)

PROMETHEUS:

Ah! Too cruel friends!

Why are you unchaining

From the depths of this dark night,

In these lucky fields, and under a sky so sweet,

These enemies of nature?

Let eternal Chaos raise between them and us

An impenetrable barrier!

Implacable hell,

Must vivify

This lovely wonder

That I knew how to create?

A favorable god

Must enflame it.

ENCELADUS:

Because you put the grandeur of your being this way

To pour boons on this new abode,

You deserve to be its sole master.

Rise to heaven, whose day you hold,

Go steal the celestial flame,

Dare create a soul

And be creator in your turn.

PROMETHEUS:

Love is in the skies; it's there I must go;

Love reigns there over the gods.

I will hurl its features, I will light its fires.

Love's the god of my heart, and I must expect all of it.

I fly to its eternal throne

On the wings of the winds.

Love carries me off to heaven.

(Prometheus flies off.)

CHORUS OF NYMPHS:

Fly, cleave the breeze, and penetrate the precincts

Of eternal palaces;

Bring back the pleasures from the abode of fear,

By spreading bounties, deserve altars.

CURTAIN

ACT II

The stage represents the same countryside. Pandora, inanimate, is on a platform. A brilliantly lit chariot descends from heaven.

A DRYAD:

Sing, wood nymphs, sing the happy return

Of the demi-god who commands the earth;

He's bringing you a new day;

He's coming back to this sweet abode

From a dwelling shining with thunder.

He's flying back to these parts in Love's chariot.

CHORUS OF NYMPHS:

What sweet aurora

Is dawning on us!

Earth, still young,

Embellish yourself.

Brilliant flowers which adorn our fields,

Summits of superb mountains

That divide the breezes, and that bear the heavens;

O burgeoning nature

Become more charming,

More worthy of her eyes!

PROMETHEUS:

(alighting from the chariot, torch in hand)

I stole it from the gods, I am bringing it to earth,

This sacred fire of tender Love,

A thousand times more powerful than that of thunder

And the fires of the day god.

CHORUS OF NYMPHS:

Daughter of heaven, soul of the world,

Enter all hearts:

The air, the earth, and the ocean

Await your favors.

PROMETHEUS:

(approaching the platform on which Pandora lies)

May this precious fire, star of nature,

May this pure flame

Number you amongst the living.

Earth, be attentive to these lucky moments.

Arise, dear thing, it's Love that commands it;

Always be obedient to her voice.

Arise, Love gives you

Life, a heart, and beautiful eyes.

(Pandora rises and walks about the stage.)

CHORUS:

Heaven! O heaven! She's breathing!

God of love, such is your sway!

PANDORA:

Where am I? And what do I see?

I never was; what power has given birth to me?

I went from nothingness to being.

What ravishing things seem to have been born with me! (a symphony is heard)

These harmonious sounds enchant my ears.

My eyes are dazzled by the accumulation of marvels

That the author of my life squanders on my heels.

Ah! Where's this coming from, that didn't appear before?

Moment by moment I think and I inform myself.

Earth, though you bear me, you are not my mother;

No question, a god is my author.

I feel him, he's talking to me, he's breathing in my heart.

Heaven! Is this me that I envisage?

The crystal of this ocean is the mirror of heaven;

Nature is painting itself; the more I see my image

The more I ought to give thanks to the gods.

NYMPHS AND TITANS:

(dancing around her)

Pandora, daughter of Love,

Burgeoning charms, novel beauty,

Be inspired forever, feel in your turn

This immortal flame

Whose life you prize. (they dance)

PANDORA:

(noticing Prometheus in the midst of the nymphs)

What object attracts my eyes!

Of all that I see in these pleasant parts

It's you, it's you, no question, to whom I owe life.

My soul is filled with the fire from your glances;

You seem still to vivify me.

PROMETHEUS:

Your beautiful eyes knew how to enflame me

Before they'd even opened;

You couldn't respond, and I dared to love you.

You speak and I adore you.

PANDORA:

You love me, dear author of my life commenced;

You love me, and I owe you my existence.

The earth enchants me: how you embellish it!

My heart flies to yours, it surrenders to its master;

And I cannot know

If my mouth has said too much or not said enough.

PROMETHEUS:

You couldn't know how to say too much, and simple nature

Speaks without sham and without deviousness.

May the future race always

Thus pronounce the name of Love. (together)

Charming Love, eternal power,

First God of my heart,

Love, your sway begins,

It's the empire of happiness.

PROMETHEUS:

Heaven! What heavy night, what bursts of thunder

Destroy the first moments

Of innocent pleasures that possess the earth!

What horror troubles my senses! (together)

Earth shakes, heaven roars,

Threatening lightning flashes

Have pierced the profound vault

Of burgeoning stars.

What power shakes the world

To its very foundations?

(A chariot can be seen descending with Mercury, Discord, Nemesis, etc.)

MERCURY:

A reckless hero has taken the celestial fire

To expiate this audacious theft.

Rise, Pandora, to the breast of the gods.

PROMETHEUS:

Cruel tyrants!

PANDORA:

Funereal order!

Tears I never knew about,

You run from my eyes.

MERCURY:

Obey, rise to heaven.

PANDORA:

Ah! I was in heaven as I saw the one I loved.

PROMETHEUS:

Cruel ones! Have pity on my extreme sorrow.

PANDORA AND PROMETHEUS:

Barbarians, stop.

MERCURY:

Come, climb to the heavens, leave:

Jupiter orders,

You must surrender

To his will.

Come, rise to the heavens, leave.

Winds, obey us and deploy your wings.

Winds, escort Pandora to the eternal vault.

(The chariot disappears.)

PROMETHEUS:

They've carried her away, jealous tyrants,

Gods, you snatch my share from me.

It was more divine than you:

You were wretched, you were enraged

By the happiness which made my work:

I'm not obliged to anyone but myself

For this precious happiness.

I made her more than Jupiter even,

I made myself loved. I vivified those beautiful eyes:

Opening, they said to me:

You love me, I love you.

She lived through me, I was living in her heart.

Jealous gods, respect our chains.

O Jupiter! O inhuman furors!

Eternal persecutor

Of the unlucky creator.

You will feel all my pains,

I will brave your power.

Your appalling lightning

Will be less formidable

Than my despairing love.

CURTAIN

ACT III

The stage represents the Palace of Jupiter, shining with gold and with light.

JUPITER:

I've seen this object on the living earth.

I've seen it and I've experienced

Transports that astonish me:

Heaven is in her eyes, the graces surround her

I feel that love has formed her.

MERCURY:

You reign, you please, and you make her tender;

You will dazzle her just-opened eyes.

JUPITER:

I was never anything but powerful and terrible:

I command in Olympus, on earth, in hell;

But hearts belong to Love.

Ah! How fate outrages me!

Though it gave me the heavens,

Though it gave me the seas,

When it divided the universe,

Love received the best share.

MERCURY:

What are you afraid of? Pandora has hardly seen the day,

And of herself, still hardly has knowledge:

Would she have felt love

From the moment of her birth?

JUPITER:

Love instructs very easily

What is Pandora incapable of?

She's a woman, she's beautiful.

There she is: let's play with her astonishment.

Let's withdraw for a moment,

Under the luminous arches of the eternal vault.

Heavens, enchant her eyes and speak to her heart.

You will deploy my grandeur and my splendor in vain.

You have nothing of the beauty she has. (he withdraws)

PANDORA:

(entering) Hardly had I experienced the dawn of life;

My eyes were opening to the day, my heart to my lover;

I had only breathed a moment.

Sweet happiness, why were you taken away?

They made me fear death:

Alas, I knew it, this threatening death:

Isn't it dying, when fate

Robs us of that which enchants us?

Gods, return me to earth and my obscurity,

That abode where I saw the lover who created me.

He twice gave me being;

I breathed, I loved: what happiness!

Hardly had I experienced the dawn of life, etc.

(All the gods with all their attributes come on stage.)

CHORUS OF GODS:

Let the stars rejoice!

Let all the gods applaud

The god of the universe!

Before him all suns blanch.

NEPTUNE:

Like the breast of the seas.

PLUTO:

The depth of hell.

CHORUS OF GODS:

Diverse worlds

Echo

With eternal concerts.

Let the stars rejoice, etc.

PANDORA:

How all that I hear conspires to terrify me!

I fear, I hate, I am fleeing from this supreme grandeur;

How hard it is to hear praise

For another god than the one I love!

THE THREE GRACES:

Daughter of charming Love,

Reign in his empire;

Earth desires you,

Heaven is your court.

PANDORA:

My eyes are offended by day which surrounds me:

Nothing pleases me, and all astonishes me.

My deserts had more attractions.

Disappear, o infinite splendor,

My lover doesn't see you. (A symphony is heard.)

Cease, useless harmony!

He doesn't hear you.

(The chorus resumes, Jupiter steps off a cloud.)

JUPITER:

New charm of nature,

Worthy of being eternal,

You cling to an earthly body, weak and mortal.

And you owe this pure and unalterable soul

To the sacred fire of heaven.

It was for the gods you were just born.

Begin to play the divinity:

Experience near your master

Happy immortality.

PANDORA:

Nothingness, from which I hardly escaped.

Is a hundred times preferable to this cruel present:

Your immortality, without the object that enchains me,

Is nothing but an immortal torture.

JUPITER:

What! You fail to recognize me as the god of thunder?

In the palace of the gods you regret the earth?

PANDORA:

Earth was my true abode

It's there I experienced love.

JUPITER:

No, you know nothing of it but an unfaithful image

In a world unworthy of it.

May love in all its entirety, may its eternal flame,

Of which you've experienced only a spark,

With all its fiery aspects embrace us today.

PANDORA:

I've experienced them all, at least I dare think so;

They equaled my tortures.

Ah! You have for yourself grandeur and glory,

Leave pleasure to lovers.

You are a god; incense must suffice for you.

You are a god, satisfy my wishes,

Console all who breathe.

A god must create happiness.

JUPITER:

I intend to make you happy, and through you, I will be.

Pleasures who follow your master,

Ministers more powerful than all the other gods,

Deploy your attractions, enchant her gorgeous eyes;

Pleasures you triumph as soon as you are known.

(The pleasures dance around Pandora and sing.)

CHORUS OF PLEASURES:

Love, love and reign with us,

The god of gods is alone worthy of you.

A VOICE:

On earth you pursue with difficulty

Pleasures flight and vain shadow;

It escapes and disgust follows.

If Zephyr pleases Flora for a moment

He withers the flowers that he blossoms;

A single day creates them and destroys them.

CHORUS:

Love, love and reign with us,

The god of gods alone is worthy of you.

A VOICE:

Immortal flowers

Are nowhere but in our fields.

Love and time

Lack wings here.

CHORUS:

Love, love, and reign with us.

The god of gods alone is worthy of you.

PANDORA:

Yes, I love, yes, sweet pleasures, you increase my flame;

But you increase my sorrow,

Charming gods, it's you who create happiness,

Go to the master of my soul.

JUPITER:

Heaven! O heaven! What!

My attentions have this fatal success?

What! I softened her soul and it's for my rival!

MERCURY:

(coming on stage) Jupiter, arm your lightning;

Take your fires, go reduce to ashes

Your audacious enemies.

Prometheus is armed, the furious Titans

Threaten the vaults of heaven.

They are heaping mountains of appalling masses:

Already their pitiless crowd

Is approaching these parts.

JUPITER:

I will punish them all. Alone, I will suffice against them.

PANDORA:

What! You will punish him, you who cause his pain?

You are nothing but an all-powerful jealous tyrant.

Love me with a love even more violent,

I will punish you with my hate.

JUPITER:

Let's march and let thunder burst before me.

PANDORA:

Cruel! Have pity of my mortal terror:

Judge of my heart, since I implore you.

JUPITER:

(to Mercury) Take care to escort Pandora.

Gods, how my heart is desolated!

I am experiencing the horrors which threaten the world.

The universe rests in a profound peace;

A beauty appears and the universe is troubled.

(Jupiter leaves.)

PANDORA:

O days of my birth! O too funereal charms!

Burgeoning desires, how you were deceived.

What! Beauty, love, and celestial favors;

All these treasures have caused my misfortunes!

Love, who caused my birth, appease all these alarms;

Aren't you sovereign of the gods?

Come dry my tears,

Enchain and disarm

Heaven and earth.

CURTAIN

ACT IV

The stage represents the Titans armed, with mountains in the background. Several giants are on the mountains, piling up rocks.

ENCELADUS:

Yes, we and our brothers, and all nature

Have felt your cruel injury.

Terrible vengeance is already in our hands.

Do you see these mountains hanging in precipices?

Do you see these rocks piled up?

They will soon be cast down

On the barbarous gods who have offended us.

We will punish the injustices

Of our jealous tyrants with our own downbeaten hands.

PROMETHEUS:

Earth, learn to defend yourself against heaven.

Drums and trumpets, organs of battles,

For the first time your sounds will make themselves heard;

Blare out, guide our steps. (they leave to the sound of trumpets)

Heaven will be the prize of your lucky courage.

Friends, I only pretend to Pandora and her faith.

Leave me this just share.

March, Titans, and follow me.

CHORUS OF TITANS:

Let's run to arms

Against these cruel gods.

Let's spread alarm

In immortal hearts.

Let's run to battles

Against these cruel gods.

PROMETHEUS:

Thunder responds in bursts to our trumpets.

(A chariot bearing the gods descends onto the mountains in the roar of thunder. Pandora is by Jupiter. Prometheus continues.)

PROMETHEUS:

Jupiter is leaving his shelter

Lightning has given the signal:

Let's begin the fatal battle.

(The giants climb.)

CHORUS OF NYMPHS:

(who border the stage)

Drums, trumpets, and thunder,

Gods and Titans, what are you doing?

With your terrible blows, you confound

Heaven, hell, and earth.

(Uproar of thunder and trumpets.)

TITANS:

Give up, tyrants of the universe,

Be punished for your cruel furors;

Fall, tyrants.

GODS:

Die, rebels.

TITANS:

Fall, come into our chains.

GODS:

Rush on to Hell.

PANDORA:

Earth, heaven, o profound sorrow!

Gods, Titans, calm my terror.

I have caused the misfortunes of the world:

Earth, heaven, all are perishing because of me.

TITANS:

Fling our spears.

GODS:

Strike, thunder.

TITANS:

Let's overthrow the gods.

GODS:

Let's destroy the earth (together).

Fall, come in to our chains

Rush on to hell.

(A great silence. A brilliant cloud descends. Destiny appears in the midst of the clouds.)

DESTINY:

Halt! Destiny who commands you all

Wills that you suspend your blows.

(Another silence.)

PROMETHEUS:

Unalterable being,

Sovereign of time,

Dictate to our tyrants

Your irrevocable order.

CHORUS:

O Destiny, speak, explain yourself;

The gods will stoop under your law.

DESTINY:

(in the midst of the gods who have assembled around him)

Cease, cease, funereal war.

This day create another universe.

Sovereigns of the celestial abode,

Return Pandora to her deserts.

Gods, heap on this object all your diverse gifts.

Titans, who right up to heaven have carried the war,

Unlucky be your lands,

Forever groan

Under these upturned mountains

That are going to fall back to the earth.

(The rocks detach themselves and fall back. The chariot of the gods descends to earth. They deliver Pandora back to Prometheus.)

JUPITER:

O Destiny! The master of the gods

Is the slave of your power.

Well! Be obeyed; but let this day begin

The eternal divorce between earth and the heavens.

Nemesis, leave these somber parts.

(Nemesis leaves and Jupiter continues.)

JUPITER:

Seduce the heart, deceive the eyes,

Of the beauty that offends me.

Pandora, know my vengeance

Right in my precious gifts.

Let this moment begin

The eternal divorce between earth and the heavens.

CURTAIN

ACT V

The stage represents a thicket through which debris of rocks are visible.

PANDORA:

(holding the box)

Eh what! Are you leaving me, dear lover that I adore?

Are you beaten or victor?

PROMETHEUS:

Victory is mine, if you still love me.

Love and destiny speak in my favor.

PANDORA:

Eh what! Are you leaving me dear lover that I adore?

PROMETHEUS:

The Titans have fallen; pity their terrible fate.

I must ease their imprisonment.

Let's teach the human race

To succor the unfortunate.

PANDORA:

Stay for a minute. Look at your victory.

Let's open this charming gift

From the sovereign of the gods.

Let's open it.

PROMETHEUS:

What are you doing? Alas, deign to believe me

I fear everything from a rival; and these curious attentions

Are new snares with which the gods will entrap you?

PANDORA:

What! You think—?

PROMETHEUS:

Think at my prayer,

Think of the interest of all of nature,

And at least await my return in these parts.

PANDORA:

Well! You wish it! You must be satisfied.

I submit my reason; I only wish to please you.

I swear, I promise by my tender love,

To always believe you.

PROMETHEUS:

You promise me?

PANDORA:

I swear by you yourself.

One obeys only that which one loves.

PROMETHEUS:

Enough of that, I am leaving, and I am reassured.

Wood nymphs, increase your zeal;

Sing of this universe destroyed and reconstructed.

Let all be embellished to her taste,

Since it was all made for her.

(Prometheus leaves.)

A NYMPH:

Here's the golden age; here's the time of pleasure

Sweet leisure, pure heaven, happy days,

Tender loves,

Nature is your mother.

How it will last forever.

ANOTHER NYMPH:

No longer will discord and miserable war

Come to afflict us;

Happiness is born on earth

Misfortune is a stranger.

Flowers are beginning to appear;

What hand could blast them?

Pleasures rush to be born;

What tyrants would make them perish?

CHORUS:

(repeating) Here's the golden age, etc.

A NYMPH:

You see the eloquent Mercury;

He is with Pandora, he confirms in these parts

On behalf of the master of the gods,

The peace of nature.

(The nymphs withdraw; Pandora comes forward with Nemesis who appears under the shape of Mercury.)

NEMESIS:

I already told you. Prometheus is jealous.

He's abusing his power.

PANDORA:

He is the author of my birth,

My king, my lover, my spouse.

NEMESIS:

He carries to excess the rights he has over you.

Ought he to forbid you forever

From seeing this charming gift that you have from the gods?

PANDORA:

He fears everything. His love is tender,

And I love to comply with his wishes.

NEMESIS:

He exacts too much, adorable Pandora;

He hasn't done for you all that you deserve.

In creating you, he could have given you beauties

That, perhaps, you still are lacking.

PANDORA:

He gave me a tender heart, he charms me, he adores me:

Could he have embellished me better?

NEMESIS:

Your charms will perish.

PANDORA:

You make me shiver!

NEMESIS:

This mysterious box

Immortalizes beauty.

By opening this enchanted treasure,

You will always be beautiful; always happy.

You will reign over your spouse;

He will be submissive and clever.

Beware of a jealous tyrant;

Create a docile subject.

PANDORA:

No, he is my lover, he must be forever.

He is my king, my god, provided he is faithful.

It's to love forever that he must be immortal.

It's to charm him better that I want more attractions.

NEMESIS:

Ah! It's too much to forbid you;

I am serving your tender loves.

I only want you to learn

How to please, to be longed for forever.

PANDORA:

But aren't you abusing my feeble innocence?

Could you have so much cruelty?

NEMESIS:

Ah, who could deceive so much beauty?

All take your defense.

PANDORA:

Alas, I would die of sorrow

If I deserved his wrath,

If I were able to displease

The master of my heart.

NEMESIS:

In the name of the whole of nature

In the name of your spouse, give me your confidence.

PANDORA:

That name does it and I believe you.

Let's open. (she opens and night spreads over the stage, and a subterranean noise is heard)

What a thick, terrifying vapor

Steals the day from me and disturbs all my senses?

Deceitful God, implacable minister!

Ah! What frightful evils I am experiencing.

I see I am guilty and punished.

NEMESIS:

Let's flee from the earth and its airs.

Jupiter is avenged, let's return to hell.

(Nemesis vanishes into the abyss; Pandora faints on a bed of grass.)

PROMETHEUS:

(arriving) O shock!

O profound sorrow!

Fatal absence! Horrible changes,

What malevolent stars

Have blasted the face of the world?

I don't see Pandora; she doesn't

Respond to the plaintive accents

Of my voice.

Pandora! Why, alas!

From the infernal shore

Unchained monsters fly through

These regions.

FURIES AND DEMONS:

(running across the stage)

The times are full;

Here's our sway;

All that breathes

Will submit to us.

Sad coldness

Freezes nature

In the northern climbs.

Trembling fear,

Arrogant insult,

Somber remorse,

Bloody war,

Arbiters of fate,

All the furies,

Go with delight

In these impious regions

To bring death.

PROMETHEUS:

What! Death has made its passage into these parts!

What! Earth has lost its eternal spring

And its wretched inhabitants

Have fallen as shares

To the fury of the gods, to hell, and to time!

These nymphs with their tears water this shore.

Pandora, dear object, my life and my image,

Masterpiece of my hands, idol of my heart,

Answer my sorrow.

I see; she lost the use of her senses.

PANDORA:

Ah! I am unworthy of you;

I've ruined the universe; I've betrayed my spouse.

Punish me: our ills are my work.

Strike.

PROMETHEUS:

Me, punish you?

PANDORA:

Strike, snatch from me

This odious life

That you made happy

That day I first saw you.

CHORUS OF NYMPHS:

Tender spouse, dry her tears.

Grant mercy to her beauty.

The excess of her frailty

Doesn't equal her charms.

PROMETHEUS:

What! Despite my prayer and despite your oaths

You opened this odious box?

PANDORA:

A cruel god with his enchantments

Seduced my weak and overcurious reason.

O fatal credulity!

All evils came out of this detested box.

All evils come from sad Pandora.

LOVE:

(descending from heaven)

All the treasures are yours.

Love still remains to you.

(The scene changes and represents the palace of love.)

LOVE:

(continuing) For you I will battle rigorous destiny.

To humans I've given Being.

They will not be unhappy

If they have only me for Master.

PANDORA:

Charming comforter, god worthy of my wishes,

You who live in me, you, the soul of my soul,

Punish Jupiter by increasing the flame

With which you inflame the two of us.

PROMETHEUS AND PANDORA:

Vainly heaven musters on us

Evils, fear, and horror of death.

We will endure together

And that is not suffering.

LOVE:

Descend, sweet Hope,

Come, flattering desires

Dwell in all hearts,

You will be their delight.

You are deceitful,

It's you they implore;

Through you they are joyful

At the moment which passes and flees

From the moment that is not yet.

PANDORA:

By destiny's formidable chains

We are enmeshed with eternal misfortunes:

But Hope, forever helpful

With her hands will come to dry our tears.

In our ills will be our delights.

We will have charming errors,

We will be on the edge of precipices,

But love will cover them with flowers.

CURTAIN

ABOUT THE TRANSLATOR

Frank J. Morlock has written and translated many plays since retiring from the legal profession in 1992. His translations have also appeared on Project Gutenberg, the Alexandre Dumas Père web page, Literature in the Age of Napoléon, Infinite Artistries.com, and Munsey's (formerly Blackmask). In 2006 he received an award from the North American Jules Verne Society for his translations of Verne's plays. He lives and works in México.

www.ingramcontent.com/pod-product-compliance
Lightning Source LLC
LaVergne TN
LVHW041625070426
835507LV00008B/451